# IS-101.C: Preparing for Federal Disaster Operations: FEMA

**By**

**Fema**

10/31/2013

# Lesson 1: Introduction to Federal Disaster Response & Recovery

## Course Welcome

This course is designed to help prepare you to support disaster operations in a federally declared incident. In recent years, we have witnessed the destruction that can be caused by the forces of nature, or precipitated by terrorist or criminal acts.

Responding to incidents requires that we must be ready, willing, and able to deploy at a moment's notice. This course provides you with practical tips and advice for incident deployment.

If you have not completed the IS 100.b, IS 200.b, IS 700.a, and IS 800.b courses, you may want to do so before completing this course.

## Course Objectives

Upon completing this course, you will be able to describe how to:

- Understand the mission, role, and organization of FEMA during Federally declared incidents.
- Identify the primary Federal partners (Emergency Support Functions) that support disaster operations.
- Prepare for deployment, including detailing what information to gather, what steps to take, and what things to pack.
- Check in when you arrive at your assigned location.
- Acclimate to the working and living conditions at the assigned incident facility.
- Take care of yourself during deployment.
- Maintain standards for accountability.
- Complete the check-out process.

## Lesson Overview

You should now be ready to start the first lesson of this course. The objectives for each of the major topics of this lesson are as follows:

- **Doctrine and Authorities**: To describe disaster response and recovery doctrine and authorities.

* **Roles:** To identify the roles of response partners.
* **Federal Assistance:**  To identify the process for requesting Federal assistance and the available programs.

# The Federal Emergency Management Agency (FEMA)

FEMA's existence represents a small part of the long history of Federal participation in emergency management. Although FEMA may be the best-known brand of Federal emergency management assistance, it is just one member of a much larger team. Other Federal departments play important roles in preparing for, responding to, recovering from, and mitigating disasters. State, Tribal, and local governments have significantly enhanced and expanded their capabilities since 2003, and communities, as always, continue to provide the first line of defense for and response to disasters and emergencies.

With a renewed emphasis on engaging the private sector, nongovernmental entities, and the general public, emergency management practitioners in the United States value collaboration as never before. Our collective experience as a Nation has created a more coordinated approach to emergency management, brought more players to the table, and demonstrated the power of teamwork.

FEMA's mission is "to support our citizens and first responders to ensure that as a Nation we work together to build, sustain, and improve our capability to prepare for, protect against, respond to, recover from, and mitigate all hazards." In pursuing this mission, all FEMA activities are based on specific authorities such as the Homeland Security Act of 2002, Robert T. Stafford Disaster Relief and Emergency Assistance Act (Stafford Act), and Homeland Security Presidential Directive-5. FEMA's activities and functions are also driven by doctrinal guidance such as the National Strategy for Homeland Security and the National Response Framework.

# Who We Serve

During an incident, we coordinate and provide services to assist a wide variety of groups and individuals. These groups include:

* The American public
* Disaster survivors
* State, tribal, territorial, and local governments
* Community and voluntary organizations

Disaster Operations require partnerships among levels of government, the private sector, and nongovernmental organizations, requiring a Whole Community approach to support the needs of disaster survivors.

# Federal Role

When an incident occurs that exceeds or is anticipated to exceed State, tribal, or local resources, the Federal Government may provide resources and capabilities to support the State response. The Federal Government maintains a wide array of capabilities and resources that can be made available upon request of the Governor.

For incidents involving primary Federal jurisdiction or authorities (e.g., on a military base or a Federal facility or lands), Federal departments or agencies may be the first responders and first line of defense, coordinating activities with State, territorial, tribal, and local partners.

The Federal Government also maintains working relationships with private-sector businesses and NGOs.

**Roles of Key Federal Officials**

**National Leadership: The President**

- Leads the Federal Government response effort.
- Ensures that the necessary coordinating structures, leadership, and resources are applied quickly and efficiently to large-scale and catastrophic incidents.
- Sets policy for large-scale incidents after consulting with the Homeland Security Council and National Security Council.

**Secretary of Homeland Security**

- Serves as the principal Federal official for domestic incident management.
- Coordinates the Federal resources utilized in the prevention of, preparation for, response to, or recovery from terrorist attacks, major disasters, or other emergencies.
- Provides the President with an overall architecture for domestic incident management and coordinates the Federal response, when required, while relying upon the support of other Federal partners.
- Contributes elements of the response consistent with the Department of Homeland Security's (DHS's) mission, capabilities, and authorities.

Note: Federal assistance for incidents that do not require DHS coordination may be led by other Federal departments and agencies consistent with their authorities. The Secretary of Homeland Security may monitor such incidents and may activate specific Framework mechanisms to provide support to departments and agencies without assuming overall leadership for the Federal response to the incident.

### FEMA Administrator

- Serves as the principal advisor to the President, the Secretary of Homeland Security, and the Homeland Security Council on all matters regarding emergency management.
- Assists the Secretary of Homeland Security to prepare for, protect against, respond to, and recover from all-hazards incidents.
- Manages the operation of the National Response Coordination Center and provides for the effective support of all Emergency Support Functions.
- Makes recommendations to the President through the Secretary of Homeland on Stafford Act declaration requests.
- Manages the core DHS grant programs supporting homeland security.

### Law Enforcement: Attorney General

- Serves as the chief law enforcement officer of the United States.
- Generally acting through the Federal Bureau of Investigation:
    - Assumes lead responsibility for criminal investigations of terrorist acts or terrorist threats by individuals or groups inside the United States or directed at U.S. citizens or institutions abroad.
    - Coordinates activities of the other members of the law enforcement community to detect, prevent, and disrupt terrorist attacks against the United States.
- Approves requests submitted by State Governors pursuant to the Emergency Federal Law Enforcement Assistance Act for personnel and other Federal law enforcement support during incidents.
- Enforces Federal civil rights laws and provides expertise to ensure that these laws are appropriately addressed.

### National Defense and Defense Support of Civil Authorities: Secretary of Defense

- Approves requests for response resources.

    The primary mission of the Department of Defense (DOD) and its components is national defense. Because of this critical role, resources are committed after approval by the Secretary of Defense or at the direction of the President. Many DOD components and agencies are authorized to respond to save lives, protect property and the environment, and mitigate human suffering under imminently serious conditions, as well as to provide support under their separate established authorities, as appropriate. The provision of defense support is evaluated by its legality, lethality, risk, cost, appropriateness, and impact on readiness.

- Retains command of military forces.

When Federal military and civilian personnel and resources are authorized to support civil authorities, command of those forces will remain with the Secretary of Defense. DOD elements in the incident area of operations and National Guard forces under the command of a Governor will coordinate closely with response organizations at all levels.

## International Coordination: Secretary of State

- Manages international preparedness, response, and recovery activities relating to domestic incidents.
- Manages efforts related to the protection of U.S. citizens and U.S. interests overseas.

## Intelligence: Director of National Intelligence

- Leads the Intelligence Community and serves as the President's principal intelligence advisor.
- Oversees and directs the implementation of the National Intelligence Program.

## Other Federal Department and Agency Heads

- Serve in primary, coordinating, and/or support roles based on their authorities and resources and the nature of the threat or incident.
- Participate as members of the Unified Coordination Group in situations where their agency or department has responsibility for directing or managing a major aspect of a response.
- Execute their own authorities to declare disasters or emergencies. For example, the Secretary of Health and Human Services can declare a public

health emergency. These declarations may be made independently or as part of a coordinated Federal response. Where those declarations are part of an incident requiring a coordinated Federal response, those Federal departments or agencies act within the overall coordination structure of the Framework.

**Note:** When the overall coordination of Federal response activities is required, it is implemented through the Secretary of Homeland Security consistent with Homeland Security Presidential Directive (HSPD) 5. Other Federal departments and agencies carry out their response authorities and responsibilities within this overarching construct. Nothing in the Framework alters or impedes the ability of Federal, State, tribal, or local departments and agencies to carry out their specific authorities or perform their responsibilities under all applicable laws, Executive orders, and directives. Additionally, nothing in the Framework is intended to impact or impede the ability of any Federal department or agency to take an issue of concern directly to the President or any member of the President's staff.

# Disaster Operations Goals

Federal response has a number of specific goals when activated for an emergency. These goals include:

- To save lives.
- To protect property and the environment.
- To ensure basic human needs are met:
    - Public health and safety,
    - Temporary shelter, and
    - Critical resources (water, food, ice, etc.).
- To restore critical infrastructure:
    - Utilities,
    - Telecommunications, and
    - Transportation.
- To restore essential Government services.

# The Federal Incident Management and Support Organizational Structure

In this part of the lesson, you will learn about the following incident organizations:

- National Response Coordination Center (NRCC)
- Regional Response Coordination Center (RRCC)

- Joint Field Office (JFO)
- Disaster Recovery Center (DRC)

# Understanding Incident Management and Support

Recently developed FEMA doctrine makes a clear distinction between Incident Management and Incident Support as it relates to Federal-level disaster operations:

- **Incident management** is the incident-level operation of the Federal role in emergency response, recovery, logistics, and mitigation. Responsibilities in incident management include the direct control and employment of resources, management of incident offices, operations, and delivery of Federal assistance through all phases of emergency response.
- **Incident support** is the coordination of all Federal resources that support emergency response, recovery, logistics, and mitigation. Responsibilities include the deployment of national-level assets, support of national objectives and programs affected during the disaster, and support of incident operations with resources, expertise, information, and guidance.

# National Response Coordination Center (NRCC)

The National Response Coordination Center (NRCC) is a multiagency center located at FEMA Headquarters. During an incident, the NRCC operates on a 24/7 basis or as required to:

- Monitor potential or developing incidents.
- Support the efforts of regional and field components, including coordinating the preparedness of national-level emergency response teams and resources.
- Initiate mission assignments or reimbursable agreements to activate other Federal departments and agencies (in coordination with Regional Response Coordination Centers).
- Activate and deploy national-level specialized teams.

In addition, the NRCC resolves Federal resource support conflicts and other implementation issues forwarded from the field.

# Regional Response Coordination Center (RRCC)

Each of FEMA's regional offices maintains a Regional Response Coordination Center (RRCC). The RRCCs are coordination centers that expand to become an interagency facility in anticipation of a serious incident or immediately following an incident.

Operating under the direction of the FEMA Regional Administrator, the RRCCs coordinate Federal regional response efforts until the Joint Field Office is established.

Regional Response Coordination Centers (RRCCs) are 24/7 interagency coordination facilities staffed in anticipation of a serious incident in the FEMA region or immediately following an incident.

After establishing communications with the affected State emergency management agency, RRCCs:

- Develop initial Federal objectives,
- Provide Federal support to the affected States, and
- Deploy teams to establish the Joint Field Office (JFO) that will assume these functions.


# One RRCC Per Region

Each of FEMA's regional offices maintains an RRCC. Regional offices are FEMA's permanent presence for communities and States across the Nation, help develop all-hazards operational plans, and generally help States and communities become better prepared.

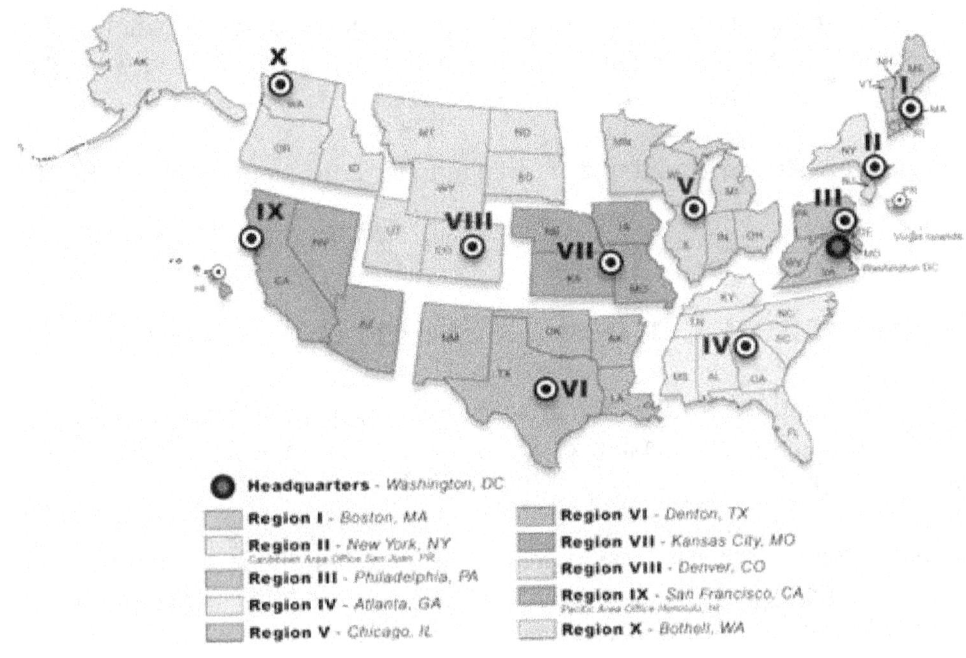


# Joint Field Office (JFO)

While FEMA has commonly referred to it as "the field," FEMA's incident level refers to the level at which FEMA incident management is accomplished, typically in partnership with States and in support of local officials.

One field facility is the Joint Field Office (JFO). The JFO:

- Is a multiagency coordination center established near the incident site.
- Provides a central location for coordination of Federal, State, local, tribal, nongovernmental, and private-sector organizations.
- Enables the effective and efficient coordination of Federal prevention, preparedness, response, and recovery activities.

The JFO is often set up in an abandoned building with folding tables for desks, shared computers, and phones. To the outside eye, it may appear chaotic as everyone pitches in and gets the job done.

The JFO may be the primary Federal incident management field structure used to coordinate Federal, State, tribal, and local governments and private-sector businesses and nongovernmental organizations (NGOs) with primary responsibility for response and short-term recovery.

Personnel from Federal and State departments and agencies, other jurisdictional entities, and private-sector businesses and NGOs may be requested to staff various levels of the JFO, depending on the requirements of the incident.

JFOs are organized, staffed, and managed in a manner consistent with NIMS principles.

# JFO Leadership: Unified Coordination Group

The Unified Coordination Group is the primary Federal or State organizational structure for managing and supporting disaster response operations at the field level. The Unified Coordination Group:

- Is comprised of senior leaders representing State and Federal interests, and in certain circumstances tribal governments, local jurisdictions, the private sector, or nongovernmental organizations.
- Applies unified command principles to coordinating assistance being provided to support the local, tribal, and State response.

# Unified Coordination Group Members

The composition of the Unified Coordination Group varies, depending upon the scope and nature of the incident. For a Stafford Act incident, two key group members include:

- **Federal Coordinating Officer (FCO).** The FCO is appointed by the President to execute Stafford Act authorities. The FCO is the primary Federal representative with whom the State, tribal, and local response officials interface to identify needs and set objectives for an effective collaborative response.
- **State Coordinating Officer (SCO).** The SCO is appointed by the Governor to coordinate State disaster assistance efforts. The SCO works with the FCO to formulate State requirements and set priorities for use of Federal support.

# Additional Unified Coordination Group Members

Additional members of the Unified Coordination Group may include the following individuals:

## Federal Resource Coordinator

In non-Stafford Act situations, when a Federal department or agency acting under its own authority has requested the assistance of the Secretary of Homeland Security to obtain support from other Federal departments and agencies, DHS may designate a Federal Resource Coordinator (FRC). In these situations, the FRC coordinates support through interagency agreements and memorandums of understanding. Relying on the same skill set, DHS may select the FRC from the Federal Coordinating Officer cadre or other personnel with equivalent knowledge, skills, and abilities. The FRC is responsible for coordinating timely delivery of resources to the requesting agency.

## Senior Federal Law Enforcement Official

The Senior Federal Law Enforcement Official (SFLEO) is an individual appointed by the Attorney General during an incident requiring a coordinated Federal response to coordinate all law enforcement, public safety, and security operations with intelligence or investigative law enforcement operations directly related to the incident. The SFLEO is a member of the Unified Coordination Group and, as such, is responsible to ensure that allocation of law enforcement requirements and resource allocations are coordinated as appropriate with all other members of the Group. In the event of a terrorist incident, the SFLEO will normally be a senior FBI official who has coordinating authority over all law enforcement activities related to the incident, both those falling within the Attorney General's explicit authority as recognized in HSPD-5 and those otherwise directly related to the incident itself.

## Defense Coordinating Officer

The Department of Defense (DOD) has appointed 10 Defense Coordinating Officers (DCOs) and assigned one to each FEMA region. If requested and approved, the DCO serves as DOD's single point of contact in the field for requesting assistance from DOD. With few exceptions, requests for Defense Support of Civil Authorities (DSCA) originating at the JFO or other field locations are coordinated with and processed through the DCO. The DCO may have a Defense Coordinating Element consisting of a staff and military liaison officers to facilitate coordination and support to activated Emergency Support Functions (ESFs).

Specific responsibilities of the DCO (subject to modification based on the situation) include processing requirements for military support, forwarding mission assignments to the appropriate military organizations through DOD-designated channels, and assigning military liaisons, as appropriate, to activated ESFs.

Note: DOD is a full partner in the Federal response to domestic incidents, and its response is fully coordinated through the mechanisms of this Framework. Concepts of "command" and "unity of command" have distinct legal and cultural meanings for military forces and military operations. For Federal military forces, command runs from the President to the Secretary of Defense to the Commander of the combatant command to the DOD on-scene commander. Military forces will always remain under the operational and administrative control of the military chain of command, and these forces are subject to redirection or recall at any time. The ICS "unified command" concept is distinct from the military chain of command use of this term. And, as such, military forces do not operate under the command of the Incident Commander or under the unified command structure.

### Joint Task Force Commander

Based on the complexity and type of incident, and the anticipated level of DOD resource involvement, DOD may elect to designate a Joint Task Force (JTF) to command Federal (Title 10) military activities in support of the incident objectives. If a JTF is established, consistent with operational requirements, its command and control element will be co-located with the senior on-scene leadership at the JFO to ensure coordination and unity of effort. The co-location of the JTF command and control element does not replace the requirement for a Defense Coordinating Officer (DCO)/Defense Coordinating Element as part of the JFO Unified Coordination Staff. The DCO remains the DOD single point of contact in the JFO for requesting assistance from DOD.

The JTF Commander exercises operational control of Federal military personnel and most defense resources in a Federal response. Some DOD entities, such as the U.S. Army Corps of Engineers, may respond under separate established authorities and do not provide support under the operational control of a JTF Commander. Unless federalized, National Guard forces remain under the control of a State Governor. Close coordination between Federal military, other DOD entities, and National Guard forces in a response is critical.

### Other Senior Officials

Based on the scope and nature of an incident, senior officials from other Federal departments and agencies; State, tribal, or local governments; and the private sector or nongovernmental organizations may participate in a Unified Coordination Group. Usually, the larger and more complex the incident, the greater the number of entities represented.

# Field-Level Leadership/Command Structure

The chart below shows the field-level leadership or command positions that may be included.

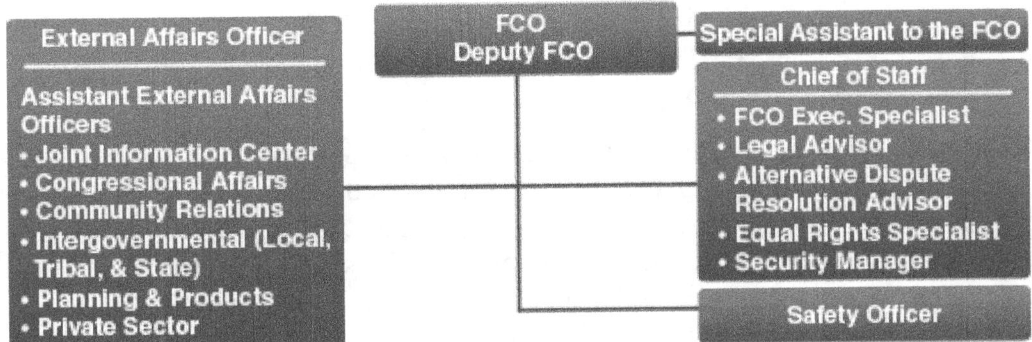


| | |
|---|---|
| **Chief of Staff** | • Manages the field-level administrative functions.<br>• Oversees efficient functioning of all staff elements.<br>• Interfaces with the FCO and Section Chiefs/staff on internal issues needing resolution.<br>• Manages FCO staff.<br>• Oversees the ongoing professional development of assigned personnel. |
| **Special Assistant to the FCO** | • Serves as a confidential advisor to the FCO.<br>• Monitors information in current situation and expected developments to identify potential risks, threats, and consequences.<br>• Assists the FCO on the development of policy and strategic planning.<br>• Oversees compliance with statutes, regulations, and other legal requirements by continually monitoring field-level operations.<br>• Organizes working sessions and meetings to analyze issues and develops optional strategies for the FCO to consider.<br>• Serves as a liaison to other Federal agencies, nongovernmental organizations, and the private sector.<br>• Represents the FCO at External Affairs events such as press conferences, VIP visits, community meetings, etc.<br>• Oversees the implementation of special projects.<br>• Identifies resources (personnel, supply, services, etc.) constraints and proposes solutions. |
| **FCO Executive Specialist** | • Establishes and maintains Federal Coordinating Officer (FCO)/Deputy FCO files.<br>• Provides administrative support to the FCO/Deputy FCO. |

|  | • Manages FCO/Deputy FCO contacts. |
| | • Serves as liaison with Section Chiefs. |

**Legal Advisor**

- Identifies potential legal issues.
- Gathers information and conducts legal research.
- Analyzes the facts, context, and the law to develop opinions, recommendations, and solutions.
- Provides legal advice, instruction, and communication.
- Prepares disaster declaration documents and resolves declaration-related issues.
- Processes external requests for information.

**Alternative Dispute Resolution Advisor**

- Provides prompt, expert means of resolving disputes and promotes conflict prevention strategies and skills at disaster sites.
- Facilitates public participation, policy making, and collaborative decision-making groups, as requested.
- Mediates legal, contract, procurement, and other complex disputes.

**Equal Rights Specialist**

- Identifies potential Equal Employment Opportunity and Civil Rights issues.
- Provides information and assistance on issues pertaining to sexual harassment, Affirmative Action, and Equal Employment Opportunity.
- Ensures nondiscrimination in hiring decisions and in staffing and managing the JFO, DRCs, and other disaster operations offices.
- Ensures that the administration and service delivery of the JFO or DRCs are conducted without regard to race, color, national origin, sex, age, religion, or physical or mental disability.

**Security Manager**

- Conducts security needs and FEMA Security Program needs assessment.
- Identifies available local law enforcement agencies and their resource capabilities.
- Sets up secure environment for personnel identification operations (i.e., badging and fingerprinting).
- Develops and implements Occupant Emergency Plan (OEP) for JFOs and other field facilities.

- Establishes and monitors security field operations.

**Safety Officer**
- Advises management officials in charge of FEMA worksites of all occupational safety and health matters.
- Assists management officials in implementation of Federal, State, tribal, and local safety and health requirements.
- Assesses local risk and determines need for FEMA safety and health programs.
- Develops the Incident Safety Plan.
- Conducts inspections, surveys, and audits to identify safety and health hazards, and makes recommendations for abatement and implementation of FEMA safety and health programs.
- Acts to respond to an emergency or prevent others' unsafe acts.

**Liaison Officer**
- Serves as the point of contact for assisting and coordinating agencies not otherwise represented at the field level.

**External Affairs Officer**

Manages all External Affairs elements including:

- **Joint Information Center (JIC):** Joint Information Center activities ensure the coordinated and timely release of incident-related prevention, preparedness, response, recovery, and mitigation information to the public.
- **Congressional Affairs:** Congressional Affairs provides information to the Washington, DC, and district offices of Members of Congress. It addresses incident-related questions, concerns, and problems expressed by their constituents.
- **Community Relations:** Community Relations program provides the vital information link between the Department of Homeland Security, Federal Emergency Management Agency, the State and local communities, and those affected by disasters.
- **Intergovernmental (State, Local, and Tribal Affairs):** State, Local, and Tribal coordination assists with direct communications interaction and outreach to public and elected officials. Tribal

Affairs provides procedures to facilitate incident management programs and resources available to tribal governments to assist them in protecting their families, community livelihood, and cultural and environmental resources.

- **Private Sector:** Private Sector coordination assists with communications involving counterparts in the nongovernmental and commercial areas.
- **Planning and Products:** Planning and Products develops all external and internal communications strategies and products for the External Affairs organization and components. This includes recognition of the need for specialized communications procedures to cover language and special needs.

# FEMA Field-Level General Staff

FEMA field operations are organized into four sections based on the Incident Command System (ICS) standard organization.

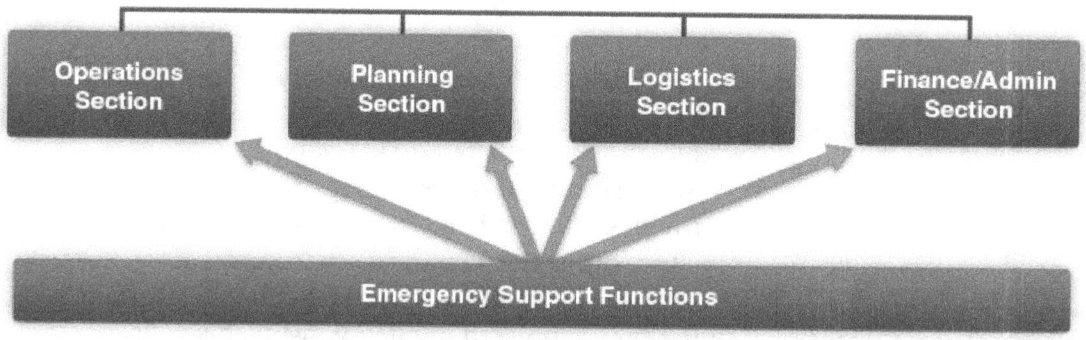


Depending on the scope and nature of the incident, the Unified Coordination Group identifies which Emergency Support Functions (ESFs) to activate based on the established objectives and incident action plan. You will learn more about ESFs later in this lesson.

# Field-Level General Staff Roles

Although the FEMA General Staff use ICS titles, their function is to support the onsite incident command structure. Below is a summary of the different roles assumed by each Section.

| Section | FEMA Field General Staff | Incident Scene General Staff |
| --- | --- | --- |
| **Operations** | The Operations Section coordinates operational support with on-scene incident management efforts. Branches, Divisions, and Groups may be added or deleted as required, depending on the nature of the incident. The Operations Section is also responsible for coordinating with other Federal facilities that may be established to support incident management activities. | The incident scene Operations Section is responsible for all tactical incident operations and implementation of the Incident Action Plan. In the Incident Command System, it normally includes subordinate Branches, Divisions, and/or Groups. |
| **Planning** | The Planning Section's functions include the collection, evaluation, dissemination, and use of information regarding the threat or incident and the status of Federal resources. The Planning Section prepares and documents Federal support actions and develops unified action, contingency, long-term, and other plans. | The incident scene Planning Section is responsible for the collection, evaluation, and dissemination of operational information related to the incident, and for the preparation and documentation of the Incident Action Plan. This Section also maintains information on the current and forecasted situation and on the status of resources assigned to the incident. |
| **Logistics** | The Logistics Section coordinates logistics support that includes: control of and accountability for Federal supplies and equipment; resource ordering; delivery of equipment, supplies, and services to the JFO and other field locations; facility location, setup, space management, building services, and | The incident scene Logistics Section is responsible for providing facilities, services, and material support for the incident. It also provides facilities, security (of the Incident Command facilities), transportation, |

| | general facility operations; transportation coordination and fleet management services; information and technology systems services; administrative services such as mail management and reproduction; and customer assistance. | supplies, equipment maintenance and fuel, food services, communications and information technology support, and emergency responder medical services, including inoculations, as required. |
|---|---|---|
| **Finance and Administration** | The Finance and Administration Section is responsible for the financial management, monitoring, and tracking of all Federal costs relating to the incident and the functioning of the FEMA field operations while adhering to all Federal laws and regulations. This Section includes Cost, Procurement, Human Resources, and Training Units. | The incident scene Finance and Administration Section is responsible for all administrative and financial considerations surrounding an incident. Some of the functions that fall within the scope of this Section are recording personnel time, maintaining vendor contracts, overseeing compensation and claims, and conducting an overall cost analysis for the incident. |

# Field-Level Organizational Structure

Below is a standard organizational structure at the field level, including the JFO:

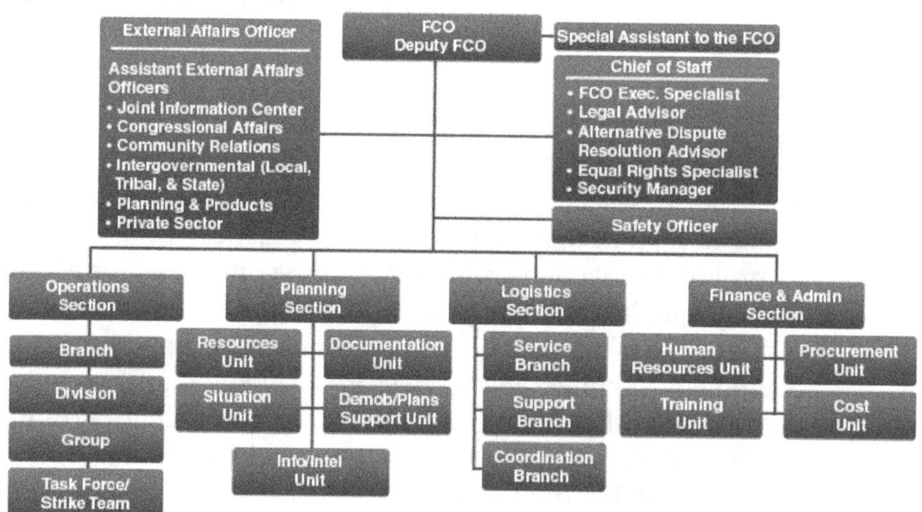

# Disaster Recovery Center (DRC)

A Disaster Recovery Center (DRC) is a readily accessible facility or mobile office where applicants may go for information about disaster assistance programs. Some of the services that a DRC may provide:

- Guidance regarding disaster recovery
- Clarification of any written correspondence received
- Answers to questions, resolution of problems, and referrals to agencies that may provide further assistance
- Status of applications being processed by FEMA.


# Emergency Support Functions Overview

Emergency Support Functions, or ESFs, are used by the Federal Government and many States as the primary mechanism to organize and provide assistance.

ESFs are organized into 14 functional areas such as transportation; public works and engineering; firefighting; search and rescue; mass care, housing, and human services; public health and medical services; agriculture and natural resources; and many more. ESFs may be selectively activated for both Stafford Act and non-Stafford Act incidents and are assigned to support headquarters, regional, and field activities.

At the Joint Field Office, these resources are assigned where needed within the Unified Coordination structure. For example, if a State requests assistance with a mass evacuation, resources from several different ESFs may be integrated into a single branch or group within the Operations Section. Regardless of where ESFs may be assigned, they coordinate closely with one another to accomplish their missions.

National Response Framework Annexes describe the scope, policies, and concept of operations of each ESF. In addition, these annexes identify ESF coordinators, primary agencies, and support agencies. Let's take a closer look at each of these roles.

An ESF coordinator has ongoing management oversight throughout the preparedness, response, and recovery phases of incident management.

A primary agency is a Federal agency with significant authorities, roles, resources, or capabilities for a particular function within an ESF. During a Stafford Act incident, the ESF primary agency serves as a Federal executive agent under the Federal Coordinating Officer.

Support agencies are those entities with specific capabilities or resources that assist the primary agency in executing the mission of the ESF.

Throughout the year, ESFs plan and prepare with all participating organizations and form partnerships with the private sector and nongovernmental organizations. In doing so, Emergency Support Functions are a key element for building our national response capability.

# Emergency Support Functions (ESFs)

Emergency Support Functions, or ESFs, are used by the Federal Government and many States as the primary mechanism to organize and provide assistance.

ESFs are organized into 14 functional areas such as transportation; public works and engineering; firefighting; search and rescue; mass care, housing, and human services; public health and medical services; agriculture and natural resources; and many more. ESFs may be selectively activated for both Stafford Act and non-Stafford Act incidents and are assigned to support headquarters, regional, and field activities.

# ESF Descriptions

The 14 ESFs are listed below:

**ESF #1: Transportation**
**ESF Coordinator: Department of Transportation**

- Aviation/airspace management and control
- Transportation safety
- Restoration and recovery of transportation infrastructure
- Movement restrictions
- Damage and impact assessment

---

**ESF #2: Communications**
**ESF Coordinator: DHS (National Communications System)**

- Coordination with telecommunications and information technology industries
- Restoration and repair of telecommunications infrastructure
- Protection, restoration, and sustainment of national cyber and information technology resources

- Oversight of communications within the Federal incident management and response structures

---

## ESF #3: Public Works and Engineering
## ESF Coordinator: Department of Defense (U.S. Army Corps of Engineers)

- Infrastructure protection and emergency repair
- Infrastructure restoration
- Engineering services and construction management
- Emergency contracting support for life-saving and life-sustaining services

---

## ESF #4: Firefighting
## ESF Coordinator: Department of Agriculture (U.S. Forest Service)

- Coordination of Federal firefighting activities
- Support to wildland, rural, and urban firefighting operations

---

## ESF #5: Emergency Management
## ESF Coordinator: DHS (FEMA)

- Coordination of incident management and response efforts
- Issuance of mission assignments
- Resource and human capital
- Incident action planning
- Financial management

---

## ESF #6: Mass Care, Emergency Assistance, Housing, and Human Services
## ESF Coordinator: DHS (FEMA)

- Mass care
- Emergency assistance
- Disaster housing
- Human services

---

## ESF #7: Logistics Management and Resource Support
## ESF Coordinator: General Services Administration and DHS (FEMA)

- Comprehensive, national incident logistics planning, management, and sustainment capability
- Resource support (facility space, office equipment and supplies, contracting services, etc.)

---

## ESF #8: Public Health and Medical Services
## ESF Coordinator: Department of Health and Human Services

- Public health
- Medical
- Mental health services
- Mass fatality management

---

## ESF #9: Search and Rescue
## ESF Coordinator: DHS (FEMA)

- Life-saving assistance
- Search and rescue operations

---

## ESF #10: Oil and Hazardous Materials Response
## ESF Coordinator: Environmental Protection Agency

- Oil and hazardous materials (chemical, biological, radiological, etc.) response
- Environmental short- and long-term cleanup

---

## ESF #11: Agriculture and Natural Resources
## ESF Coordinator: Department of Agriculture

- Nutrition assistance
- Animal and plant disease and pest response
- Food safety and security
- Natural and cultural resources and historic properties protection
- Safety and well-being of household pets

**ESF #12: Energy**
**ESF Coordinator: Department of Energy**

- Energy infrastructure assessment, repair, and restoration
- Energy industry utilities coordination
- Energy forecast

---

**ESF #13: Public Safety and Security**
**ESF Coordinator: Department of Justice**

- Facility and resource security
- Security planning and technical resource assistance
- Public safety and security support
- Support to access, traffic, and crowd control

---

**ESF #14—Superseded by National Disaster Recovery Framework**

---

**ESF #15: External Affairs**
**ESF Coordinator: DHS**

- Emergency public information and protective action guidance
- Media and community relations
- Congressional and international affairs
- Tribal and insular affairs

# ESF Activation

ESFs may be selectively activated for both Stafford Act and non-Stafford Act incidents. Not all incidents requiring Federal support result in the activation of ESFs.

For Stafford Act incidents, the National Response Coordination Center (NRCC) or Regional Response Coordination Center (RRCC) staff may activate specific ESFs by directing appropriate departments and agencies to initiate the actions delineated in the ESF Annexes.

The ESFs deliver a broad range of technical support and other services at the regional and field levels, as required by the incident.

# ESFs Within the Field Structure

Resources coordinated through ESFs are assigned where they are needed within the response structure.

For example, if a State requests assistance with a mass evacuation, resources from several different ESFs may be integrated into a single Branch or Group within the Operations Section. During the response, these resources would report to a supervisor within the assigned Branch or Group.

Regardless of where ESFs may be assigned, they coordinate closely with one another to accomplish their missions.

# Summary

This lesson presented an overview of the response doctrine and authorities, response partner roles, and Federal assistance. You should now be able to:

- Understand FEMA's role at the Federal-level of disaster operations
- Understand FEMA's Incident Management and Support structures and identify key organizational elements
- Identify the Emergency Management Support Functions (ESFs) and understand how they support disaster operations.

In the next lesson you will learn about response organizations.

# Lesson 2: Pre-Deployment and Check-In

## Lesson Overview

This lesson describes steps to take before deployment, as well as at check-in.

**Objective:** At the completion of this lesson, you will be able to describe how to prepare for deployment, including the information to gather and steps to take.

## What To Expect

**Josie**

I was recently deployed to help a tribe in the Southwest deal with damage to a fragile historic ruin caused by a flood. This was my first deployment, and, frankly, I was a little apprehensive at the beginning. When I first walked into the Joint Field Office it was like the first day of day of school at a new high school. People seemed to know each other real well from past disasters and the acronyms were a bit hard to follow. But I soon realized I needed to read the situation reports, observe, and then ask questions. If you do your homework, people are happy to slow down and help you out.

**Kamal**

Overall, my first deployment was a great experience. I made a real difference and got to meet people from other agencies. However, it was frustrating at first. With so many people from different agencies, we needed to take time to establish common procedures. I was anxious to get out into the field to begin work. In the end, the time spent working out our procedures turned out to be worthwhile. I would say that having patience and being flexible are critical when you are deployed.

**Rose**

I missed my granddaughter's first birthday party but the opportunity to help disaster survivors made the deployment worth it. In those first days, I must have helped hundreds of people sign up for food stamps. A lot of people didn't realize that we have different rules for disaster food stamps. People may qualify who normally don't. So it was very gratifying to help others. It was also draining to hear so many sad stories.

**Jim**

I was assigned to work in the Joint Information Center, or JIC. The JIC is the nerve center for public information in a disaster situation. Spokespersons from Federal and

State agencies-and the Red Cross-were all in the JIC. It was the first time I worked in a JIC and it turned out to be an excellent place to get our messages about crop loss, damage to agribusiness, and insurance issues to the public. But I do have to admit that the pace and hours were exhausting. During the first weeks, we worked 12 hours a day, 7 days a week. The veterans from other disasters seemed to thrive in this rapid-fire environment. After the first day or so, I was able to pace myself and work the long hours.

**Robert**

I was assigned to a Community Relations team. The deployment affected me emotionally a lot more than I anticipated. I talked to so many people who lost everything. I wished I could do more. But I was glad that I could give them hope that help was on the way. I learned that after a disaster, people want information almost as much as food and water. They are desperate to know what will happen to them, what help they can expect. Everyone I worked with cared about victims. They worked long hours, and they did their best to reach every eligible resident and business owner. I was happy to be part of that team.

# Pre-Deployment Information

During the initial deployment call, you should gather the following information:

- Job assignment.
- Destination including the address, contact person, phone numbers, reporting time, and directions.
- Lodging, travel, and transportation arrangements made through your agency travel office.
- Attire preference and clothing needs.

You should never self-deploy to an incident; in other words, you should never travel to a disaster site without receiving proper authorization.

Click on the Job Aid title to review the FEMA Deployment Information Guide or the FEMA Employee Deployment Checklist.

# Personal Go-Kit

If you're going to be deployed for any length of time, especially in a major disaster, prepare a go-kit with basic supplies.

Don't assume you'll find these items at your destination. Chances are good that a huge disaster like a hurricane is going to block roads and shut down the stores. That makes it very tough to put your hands on what you need if you're out there in the first days after a disaster.

# Common Personal Items for Deployment

Scroll through the list of personal items that you may want to take with you when deployed.

### Toiletries

☐ Alcohol-based hand sanitizer
☐ Toilet paper
☐ Sunblock (SPF 15 or higher) - if appropriate
☐ Insect repellent containing DEET - if appropriate
☐ Common medical items (aspirin, first aid items, antacids, eye drops, nasal spray, insect bite lotion,
   antifungal foot powder, etc.)
☐ Prescription medication
☐ Extra pair of prescription glasses, copy of prescription, and eyeglasses repair kit
☐ Contact lenses, lens case, lens cleaner, saline solution, and eyeglasses protective case
☐ Comb and brush
☐ Toothbrush, toothpaste, and dental floss
☐ Skin moisturizer, soap, and shampoo
☐ Lip balm
☐ Razor, extra blades*, and shaving cream
☐ Deodorant
☐ Scissors, nail clippers, and tweezers*
☐ Q-tips, cotton swabs
☐ Feminine hygiene products

### Clothing

☐ A 1-week supply of comfortable clothing to match the weather conditions
☐ Long pants
☐ Long- and short-sleeved shirts, sweaters (as appropriate)
☐ Hat and bandana/long neckerchief
☐ Boots or sturdy shoes and extra laces
☐ Thick socks
☐ Shower shoes
☐ Jacket and rain (or snow) gear

☐ Towel (highly absorbent, travel towels if possible) and washcloth

☐ Gloves (leather gloves if physical labor will be performed; rubber gloves if handling contaminants)

**Activities of Daily Living**

☐ Sunglasses

☐ Waterproof watch

☐ Flashlight and spare batteries

☐ Security/money belt

☐ Cash or Traveler's Checks (Power is needed to make credit card payments.)

☐ Cell phone (with charger) and list of phone numbers/addresses

☐ Ziplock bags

☐ Three Meals Ready to Eat (MREs) or other nonperishable meals (ask if needed)

☐ Portable water purifier (ask if needed)

☐ Small sewing kit

☐ Sleeping bag and pad if you have room (ask if needed)

☐ Item(s) of comfort (e.g., family photo, spiritual material)

☐ Travel alarm clock

☐ Travel pillow

☐ Large plastic garbage bags (for protecting items from rain and moisture)

*packed in checked baggage

# Get Your Personal Affairs in Order

If you are deployed for weeks, or even months, you need to have a system in place to take care of your personal affairs back home.

Some logistics to take care of before deploying include:

- Arranging for mail delivery.
- Arranging for payment of monthly bills.
- Canceling appointments.
- Letting family and friends know you are leaving.

It is important to make all needed arrangements so that your family, partner, roommates, pets, and/or plants are able to carry on without you. You will not be able to perform effectively at the incident site if you are worried about household and family matters.

# Bring Along Needed Work-Related Items

Most field offices are well stocked with supplies. However, early in a major disaster, supplies may be scarce. Scroll through the list of work-related items that you may want to take with you when deployed. When traveling by air, you will need to check with the airline to determine the luggage weight limitations.

**Office Supplies**

- ☐ Paper and pens
- ☐ Paperclips and tape
- ☐ Scissors
- ☐ Stamps
- ☐ USB memory device
- ☐ Laptop (Computers may be available, so check to see if a laptop is necessary.)

**Documents and Files**

- ☐ Hardcopies of all critical files, checklists, procedures, and information
  (There may not be power or time to print out critical information.)
- ☐ Electronic copies of forms, samples, and information
- ☐ Personal and professional address book and contact information
- ☐ Personal documentation (power of attorney, living will, insurance card, emergency contact card,
  license, Government ID, passport—if needed)

**Tools of the Trade**

- ☐ Specialized tools and equipment related to your assignment
- ☐ Safety equipment (safety goggles, gloves, hardhat, earplugs, etc.)
- ☐ Camera, film, camcorder (if required for assignment)


# Gather Information Before Deployment

Take steps to avoid unpleasant surprises. If time permits, you may want to research:

- **Directions and Maps:** Web sites such as mapquest.com or maps.google.com are excellent sources for local maps and driving directions.
- **Weather Conditions:** Check the National Weather Service or Weather Channel to determine current and projected weather conditions.
- **Situation Reports:** Ask your agency contact if you can access incident situation reports online.
- **News Reports:** Review the news reports. Be aware that initial media reports from an incident are often incomplete and based on limited information.

# Check-In Process

Your first responsibility is to complete the check-in process at the assigned incident facility (Joint Field Office, Disaster Recovery Center, etc.). You should:

- Check in with Human Resources Unit/Deployment Support staff upon arrival.
- Contact the Deployment Unit at 888-853-9648 to check in.
- Complete check-in procedures at your duty station to obtain additional information.
- Complete appropriate Federal waiver forms (retired Federal annuitants only).
- Report to the Logistics Helpdesk to obtain requisition for accountable property and network access.
- Obtain authorization for accountable property from your supervisor.
- Locate your assigned workspace.

After checking in (if time permits), you should contact your family to let them know you've arrived safely.

# Individual's Responsibilities for Government-Furnished Equipment

After you check in, you will be issued the equipment you need to complete your assignment. It is your responsibility to properly use, care for, and protect all Government property. When receiving equipment you should examine and inventory each item to make sure it is all in your possession and in working order.

In the case of any loss, theft, damage, destruction, or misuse of equipment, you must report it immediately to your supervisor and the Accountable Property Specialist within the Logistics Section. You should cooperate with any investigations of lost or stolen items.

During check-out, you must return all issued equipment. **You may be monetarily liable if you are negligent in performing these responsibilities.**

# Current Incident Status

You should obtain current incident status information through reading reports and attending briefings. This should include:

- Disaster-specific information
- Key stakeholders and personnel
- Administrative matters

More information on these administrative matters will be presented in a later lesson.

# Review Current Incident Status Information/Initial Briefing

Next, make sure you obtain current incident status information through reports and by attending briefings. Review the following list of status information you may want to collect.

**Current Incident Status Information**

☐ Damage assessments and maps
☐ Continuing threats
☐ Types of declarations, assistance, etc.
☐ Current Federal involvement in incident/emergency
☐ Key stakeholders (i.e., local, State, and other Federal agencies)
☐ Organizational chart
☐ Key personnel (name, position, locations, phone numbers, etc.)
☐ Current Incident Action Plan, including objectives and tactics
☐ Sensitive issues and concerns
☐ Recordkeeping and reporting requirements
☐ Work schedule
☐ Security policies, concerns, and procedures
☐ Safety and health concerns, policies, and procedures
☐ Cost accounting and resource tracking procedures

If your supervisor is not available to provide the above information, see if the Planning Section has any reports you can read.

# Follow Incident Command Principles

Once deployed, you should always follow these basic Incident Command Principles:

- Only take direction from your immediate supervisor.
- No freelancing.

- Don't go around the chain of command.
- Report critical information.
- Maintain awareness of potential hazards.
- Submit all required reports on time.
- Expect change in supervisors.
- Ask for help.

## Incident Command System (ICS) Principles

All incident responders must follow Incident Command System principles. Review the important ICS principles below.

### Unity of Command

- **Only take direction from your immediate supervisor.** You are assigned to a single supervisor. This supervisor may be a Division Supervisor rather than someone within your cadre. Make sure you know who your assigned supervisor is.
- **No freelancing.** If the plan is not working or your assigned activity cannot be completed, tell your supervisor. Do not create your own plan of action. Creativity is welcomed but it needs to be part of the plan!
- **Don't go around the chain of command.** Exchange of information is encouraged; however, all assignments and resource requests must go through your immediate supervisor. Even if you think there is a quicker way to get something done, wait and go through your supervisor.

### Communicate and Document

- **Report critical information** to your supervisor about status, changing conditions/needs within assigned areas, and resource needs. Let your supervisor know about resources/assets being underutilized. In others words, if you are not busy let someone know!
- **Maintain awareness of potential hazards.** Immediately let your coworkers and supervisor/lead know of any safety issues. Unity of Command/Chain of Command does not prevent you from reporting safety issues.
- **Submit all required reports** on time and make sure that they are complete and accurate.

### Span of Control: What Does This Mean?

A span of control of one supervisor to five to seven staff members is the goal.

- **Expect change.** The team you begin working with may be reconfigured to maintain span of control.
- **Ask for help.** If you are a supervisor and find that you are not able to track the activities of the personnel assigned, you may need to ask for additional levels of

supervision to be added. It is better to ask for help than to try juggling too much.

# Take Care of Your Emotional Health

While on deployment, you may encounter loss of life, serious injuries, missing and separated families, and destruction of whole areas. This stress can be dangerous to your emotional health.

Typical reactions include:

- Profound sadness, grief, and anger.
- Not wanting to leave the scene until the work is finished.
- Overriding stress and fatigue with dedication and commitment.
- Denying the need for rest
  and recovery time.

**Stress in the Disaster Recovery Environment**

Disaster work can be rewarding, but it is also stressful. It is not uncommon for disaster workers to experience stress-related problems and symptoms. These symptoms are often normal and generally temporary.

**Identifying your stress symptoms**

The checklist below lists some of the symptoms of stress. Check off all the symptoms that apply to you. You may experience multiple symptoms.

☐ Mood swings

☐ Loss of temper, irritability

☐ Tiredness or fatigue

☐ Change in appetite

☐ Difficulty in sleeping

☐ Cynicism or negativity

☐ Self-criticism

☐ Repetitious thoughts

☐ Forgetfulness

☐ Sadness or easy tearfulness

☐ Tension or anxiety

☐ Headaches and/or back pain

☐ Nausea

☐ Difficulty concentrating

☐ Self-doubt or guilt

☐ Changes in sexual energy

**Coping with stress**

The first step in coping with stress-related problems is to *acknowledge the feeling of stress*. If the stress starts to get to you, talk to someone you trust about it and try some of the stress-reducers listed below.

**Tips to reduce stress**

- Develop a personal stress relief program.
- Learn your personal signals for when things are too stressful.
- Develop a balance between home, work, spiritual, and recreational life.
- Maintain a sense of humor, develop positive attitudes, and learn to turn negatives into positives.
- Get regular rest.
- Eat smaller meals more frequently.
- Drink more water and substitute juice for soft drinks.
- Avoid caffeine, nicotine, sugar, alcohol, chocolate, and high-fat foods.
- Eat healthy foods, especially vegetables, fruits, and grains.
- Take a brief stretch and walk around during breaks, especially if you are doing repetitive tasks.
- Nurture and reward yourself by doing something nice for yourself.
- Do deep breathing exercises or meditation.
- Remove yourself from anger and conflict, if possible, until things settle down.
- Retain your sense of humor and remain positive or seek perspective about your situation.

**Beware of negative coping behaviors**

Some individuals engage in behaviors that they think will help them cope, but actually are destructive and can undermine the quality of their lives and interfere with their ability to work during the disaster period. These behaviors include:

- Abusing alcohol and drugs.
- Overeating and eating sugar and junk food.
- Neglecting health and good grooming habits.
- Behaving recklessly.
- Isolating oneself from social interaction.
- Abusing caffeine.

**Recognizing signs of stress in disaster survivors**

You may be exposed to the intense emotions of many disaster survivors. It is your job to remain sensitive to the disaster survivors' emotional state while remaining focused on your role as assistance provider. However, you are not a counselor and should not try to counsel disaster survivors. Refer disaster survivors who may need counseling to the appropriate crisis counseling group or agency.

Remember that some JFO employees may be hired from the local community and may be disaster survivors themselves.

# Summary

In this lesson, you learned about preparing for deployment and the check-in process. Make sure you know your assigned duties by:

- **Reviewing Written Materials:** Begin by reviewing all written documentation, including Incident Action Plans, relevant Position Task Books, position description, standard operating procedures, field operations guide, etc.
- **Meeting With Your Supervisor:** Discuss your responsibilities, delegations of authority, work schedules, and performance expectations.
- **Knowing Your Limits:** Disaster assistance eligibility is complex. If you are asked about a program, refer the individual to the helpline. Also, never speak to the press unless you've been authorized to do so.
- **Getting Oriented:** Get oriented to the facility layout, phone system, computers, and office support. Identify the location of the emergency exits.

The next lesson discusses timekeeping and other administrative procedures, as well as safety and security requirements.

# Lesson 3:

# Accountability, Safety, and Security

## Lesson Overview

This lesson describes accountability procedures, as well as safety and security requirements. The objectives for each of the major topics of this lesson are as follows:

- **Accountability:** To describe the administrative steps to take while deployed.
- **Safety:** To identify worker safety guidelines.
- **Security:** To describe key security procedures to follow.

## Accountability

Being accountable for one's actions during incident operations is essential. Accountability is important to protect lives and safeguard taxpayer dollars.

Accountability means abiding by established policies and guidelines, including:

- Reporting Changes
- Recording Time and Attendance
- Complying With Travel Rules
- Communicating Information and Writing Reports
- Reporting Fraud, Waste, and Abuse

The next screens present additional procedures for ensuring accountability.

## Reporting Changes

You are responsible for ensuring that your contact information remains accurate. You must:

- Notify HR Unit, Deployment Unit, and your onsite supervisor if there are changes in Duty station/assignment and lodging.
- Notify Deployment Unit for any changes in your Emergency contact information.

# Recording Time and Attendance

Throughout your deployment, you should:

- Keep track of your hours.
- Obtain authorization in advance of any overtime. Remember that any overtime must be authorized in advance.
- Report your hours per your agency policy.

**Tips on Completing Timesheets**

Whether you are a FEMA employee or an employee with another agency or organization:

- Reporting accurate time is the responsibility of each employee.
- It may be necessary to report time using a form and handwriting your information, getting it signed by your supervisor, and handing in to the appropriate office.

**Handwritten Entries**

If handwriting your information on a form:

- Complete all information blocks.
- Print clearly.
- Use blue or black pen, not a pencil.
- Give accurate contact information for your timekeeper, including the timekeeper's fax number.
- Provide a contact phone number for yourself in case there are questions.
- Sign and date your timesheet.
- Have your supervisor sign and date your timesheet.

**Automated Entries**

- **FEMA:** If using an automated system, obtain training from the Training Unit if you are unsure of any part of the system and need assistance. Note: FEMA uses WebTA automated timekeeping system.
- **Other Agencies:** You should seek guidance on the automated timekeeping system in use.

- **Printing and Signing:** Reporting policy may require that a printed screen is signed by the employee and supervisor.

### General Tips Regardless of Method

- Receive guidance on travel time, approved working hours per day, and other local policies from the "FCO Policy and Procedure Memorandum" for each specific FEMA field-level organization.
- If you work 5 hours or more, you must enter at least 30 minutes for lunch, whether you actually take the time or not. If your lunch break is more than 30 minutes, enter the actual time.
- Keep a copy for yourself of your completed forms.
- Ensure that the completed form is handed in to the appropriate office/staff person on time.

# Preparing and Submitting Travel Vouchers

Individual agency regulations should be followed for travel vouchers. In general, you must:

- Prepare and submit travel vouchers every two weeks, if on extended travel. This will assist with paying your Agency issued Travel Charge Card account in a timely manner.
- Submit a travel voucher for approval within 5 days after completion of travel.

When you are released from your assignment, your final voucher may be prepared at the JFO or other field facility before you leave. You should mail in your final voucher with any remaining receipts within 5 days of being released.

# Complying With Government Charge Card Policies

A Government issued Travel Card is provided for use only while in official travel status. Remember that a Government Credit Card may be used **only**:

- By the individual authorized to use the card.
- For official travel and travel-related business expenses that are eligible for reimbursement.
- During the designated period of travel.

# Retaining Expenditure Receipts

For proper reimbursement the following receipts are required:

- Common-carrier invoice (e.g., airline)
- Lodging receipts with a zero balance
- Rental car receipt with traveler identified as the renter
- Travel Management Center (TMC) fee
- Any other expenses over $75

Remember to submit these receipts with your travel voucher for reimbursement.

# Communicating Information

Communicating information during a deployment is critical. Effective information flow helps to:

- Improve incident safety.
- Allow effective, consistent, and timely decisions at both the tactical and strategic levels.
- Ensure consistency of messages shared with disaster survivors, agency leaders, the media, Congress, the public, and others.

# Reporting Fraud, Waste, and Abuse

Fraud, waste, and abuse of Government property and assets jeopardize our ability to achieve our mission. Even the smallest digression can delay services to disaster survivors and erode the country's trust and confidence in our Government.

If you suspect fraud, waste, or abuse, it is your duty to contact:

DHS Office of the Inspector General
Hotline: 1-800-323-8603
Fax: (202) 254-4292
Email: DHSOIGHOTLINE@dhs.gov

Complaints may be made anonymously, and you may request confidentiality.

# Ensuring a Safe Deployment

As part of FEMA's commitment to safety, the Safety Officer is responsible for and assigned to develop measures for employee safety.

The Safety Officer:

- Assesses and ensures safety conditions for employees at the JFO and for those who may be working in the field.
- Conducts safety inspections and makes recommendations for the implementation of FEMA safety and health programs.
- Presents incident-specific briefings on potential risks and hazards.
- Responds to accidents, illnesses, injuries, and other incident emergencies.

The Safety Officer depends on each person being vigilant for hazards and taking needed precautions.

# Understanding Working Conditions

### Josie

I was told that most conditions at most deployments were not as harsh as those I experienced. The weather was extremely hot and humid. Many hotels in the area were damaged. We had to take what we could find. Some workers actually slept in their cars. I was lucky. At least I had a cot. I stayed in a field tent set up by the Forest Service. They did a great job making us feel comfortable and cared for.

### Robert

FEMA work was a little more casual than I expected. People were a lot more informal than I am used to. Plus my team leader was abruptly transferred to work on a disaster in another State. Things were constantly in flux. I realized that I needed to be very flexible and just go with the flow.

### Rose

I was assigned to a station in the Disaster Recovery Center, or DRC. It was just a metal table. I had to make my own food stamp sign. We worked long hours. In the early days when we had a lot of visitors, there wasn't much free time. I usually brought a sandwich from my hotel so I could take a quick lunch break without leaving the DRC. We did have soda and snack vending machines in the break room, and the DRC was supplied with bottled drinking water. For the first week, we had to use portable toilets until the water came back on. After a while the DRC become much less busy and I was even bored at times.

# Following General Safety Guidelines

During your deployment you should ensure the safety and welfare of yourself and coworkers. Make sure to:

- Comply with all FEMA and all Occupational Safety and Health standards.
- Report all accidents to your supervisor and the Safety Officer.
- When driving, always buckle up, and drive defensively.
- Be familiar with emergency procedures for fire, bomb threats, and severe weather alerts. Know your evacuation routes and nearest hospitals, and make all emergency numbers readily accessible.
- Keep floor areas dry and clean. Watch for extension cords, computer cables, and wiring that may lead to a trip and fall injury.
- Do not lift or move heavy items without a material handling aid or assistance from another employee.

If you have a concern about a potentially hazardous situation, inform your supervisor or the Safety Officer.

# Mitigating Incident-Specific Hazards

The hazards may vary greatly from one incident to the next. Also, you may be deployed to a location that has not sustained any damage. Listed below are potential hazards that may be encountered in areas that have sustained severe damage. Scroll through the hazards and mitigation measures.

| Potential Hazard | Mitigation Measures |
| --- | --- |
| **Heat Stress and Dehydration** | - **Drink Plenty of Fluids:** During hot weather you will need to increase your fluid intake, regardless of your activity level. Don't wait until you're thirsty to drink. During heavy exercise in a hot environment, drink two to four glasses (16-32 ounces) of cool fluids each hour. Warning: If your doctor generally limits the amount of fluid you drink or has you on water pills, ask how much you should drink while the weather is hot. |

Don't drink liquids that contain alcohol, or large amounts of sugar—these actually cause you to lose more body fluid. Also avoid very cold drinks, because they can cause stomach cramps.

- **Wear Appropriate Clothing and Sunscreen:** Choose lightweight, light-colored, loose-fitting clothing. Sunburn affects your body's ability to cool itself and causes a loss of body fluids. If you must go outdoors, protect yourself from the sun by wearing a wide-brimmed hat (also keeps you cooler) along with sunglasses, and by putting on sunscreen of SPF 15 or higher (the most effective products say "broad spectrum" or "UVA/UVB protection" on their labels) 30 minutes prior to going out. Reapply sunscreen as needed.

**Heat Emergencies**

- **Pace Yourself:** If you are not accustomed to working or exercising in a hot environment, start slowly and pick up the pace gradually. There are three common heat-related emergencies: heat cramps, heat exhaustion, and heat stroke.

  Heat cramps involves heavy perspiration resulting in a loss of salts from the body. Symptoms include muscle cramps (usually in the legs and abdomen), exhaustion, and sometimes dizziness.

  Heat exhaustion is a form of shock brought about by fluid and salt loss. Heat exhaustion, if not treated, may develop into heat stroke. Signs and symptoms may include rapid, shallow breathing; weak pulse; cold and clammy skin; heavy perspiration; total body weakness; dizziness; and possible unconsciousness. Emergency care must be provided immediately.

  Heat stroke occurs when a person's temperature-regulating mechanism fails and the body cannot rid itself of excessive heat. The patient usually stops sweating. Other signs and symptoms may include dry, hot skin; loss of consciousness (possible coma); and seizures or muscular twitching. Emergency care must be provided immediately.

- **Know the Warning Signs:** If exertion in the heat makes your heart pound and leaves you gasping for breath, STOP all activity. Get into a cool area—or at least into the shade—and rest, especially if you become light-headed, confused, or weak. Let someone know that you are not feeling well.

- **Use a Buddy System:** When working in the heat, monitor the condition of your coworkers and have someone do the same for you. Heat-induced illness can cause a person to become confused or lose consciousness.

**Cold Emergencies**

- **Avoid Prolonged Exposure to Cold Temperatures:** Hypothermia is most likely at very cold temperatures, but it can occur even at cool temperatures (above 40°F) if a person becomes chilled from rain, sweat, or submersion in cold water. Frostbite causes a loss of feeling and color in affected areas and can lead to permanent damage.

- **Know the Warnings Signs:** Shivering, exhaustion, confusion, fumbling hands, memory loss, slurred speech, and drowsiness. At the first signs of redness or pain in any skin area, get out of the cold or protect any exposed skin—frostbite may be beginning. Any of the following signs may indicate frostbite: a white or grayish-yellow skin area, skin that feels unusually firm or waxy, or numbness. Never attempt to warm a frostbite area by rubbing. Seek emergency care as soon as possible.

**Poisonous Snakes**

- **Be Alert:** After a flood, storms, or hurricane, snakes are forced into places where they usually are not found. Take the following precautions if you are deployed to an area where poisonous snakes are common. Be alert for snakes in unusual places. They may be found in or around homes, barns, outbuildings, driftwood, levees, dikes, dams, stalled automobiles, piles of debris, building materials, trash, or any type of rubble or shelter. Search the premises thoroughly for snakes before beginning any cleanup or rescue operations. Snakes may be under or near any type of protective cover.

- **Wear Gloves and Use Tools:** In rescue or cleanup operations, wear heavy leather or rubber high-topped boots, and heavy gloves. Wear trouser legs outside boots. Be extremely careful around debris. Use rakes, pry bars, or other long-handled tools when removing debris. Never expose your hands, feet, or other parts of your body in a place where a snake might hide.

**Insects and Spiders**

- **Know the Risk:** Rain and flooding in a hurricane area may lead to an increase in numbers of mosquitoes, which can carry diseases such as West Nile virus or dengue fever. In most cases, the mosquitoes will be pests but will not carry communicable diseases. For more information on West Nile virus, see CDC's West Nile virus Web site.

- **Protect Yourself:** To protect yourself from mosquitoes, use screens on dwellings; wear long pants, socks, and long-sleeved shirts; and use insect repellents that contain DEET or Picaridin. When working around abandoned buildings or debris piles, stay on the lookout for spiders. If bitten by a spider, seek emergency medical attention.

**Electrical Hazards**

- **Exercise Extreme Caution:** Assume all power lines are hot unless positive confirmation is received to the contrary from a qualified electrician or utility company representative. Do not drive through standing water if downed power lines are in the water.

  If a power line falls across your car, stay inside the car and continue to drive away from the line. If the engine stalls, do not turn off the ignition. Ask someone to call the local utility company and emergency services.

- **Know the Damage Posed by Generators:** If a portable generator is improperly sized, installed, or operated, it can send power back to the electrical lines (referred to as backfeed). Backfeed can seriously injure or kill repair workers or people in neighboring buildings.

**Contaminated Drinking Water and Food**

- **Know the Source of Your Drinking Water:** After flooding conditions or extended power outages, assume all water is contaminated unless you saw the bottle it came from. Municipal water supplies in severely storm-damaged areas also are likely contaminated.

- **Wash Your Hands Frequently:** Cleaning your hands often, using soap and water (or waterless alcohol-based hand rubs when soap is not available and hands are not visibly soiled), removes potentially infectious material from your skin and helps prevent disease transmission.

**Floodwaters**

- **Heed Flash Flood Warnings:** Flash floods can come rapidly and unexpectedly. They can occur within a few minutes or hours of excessive rainfall, or when a dam or levee fails, or even due to a sudden release of water previously held by an ice or debris jam.

- **Never Cross Floodwaters:** Even if the water appears shallow enough to cross, do not attempt to cross a flooded road. Water can conceal dips, or worse, floodwaters can damage roadways. Remember, 6 inches of water will reach the bottom of most passenger cars, causing loss of control or possible stalling. One foot of water will float many vehicles.

- **Don't Allow Skin Exposure:** Leptospirosis and other disease may occur in individuals who wade, swim, or bathe in contaminated floodwaters.

**Mold**

- **Know How Exposure Affects Your Health:** After natural disasters, such as hurricanes and floods, excess moisture and standing water contribute to the growth of mold in homes and other buildings. People with asthma, allergies, or other respiratory conditions may be sensitive to mold. Proper respiratory protection should be worn when you are exposed to areas containing mold.

**Hazardous Materials**

- **Use Personal Protective Equipment as Instructed:** Disasters resulting in massive structural collapse can cause the release of chemical or biologic contaminants (e.g., asbestos or arthrospores leading to fungal infections). Persons with chronic pulmonary disease may be more susceptible to adverse effects from these exposures. If working in potentially contaminated areas, avoid skin contact or inhalation of vapors by properly using the protective clothing and respirators assigned to you by your supervisor or the Safety Officer.

- **Exercise Caution Moving Unknown Objects:** Floodwaters can dislodge tanks, drums, pipes, and equipment, which may contain hazardous materials such as pesticides or propane. Do not attempt to move unidentified dislodged containers without first

contacting the local fire department or hazardous
materials team.

- **Wash Your Hands:** Frequently and thoroughly wash
  skin areas that may have been exposed to pesticides and
  other hazardous chemicals.

**Damaged Structures**

- **Assume Damaged Structures Are Unstable:**
  Floodwaters, tornadoes, earthquakes, or other forces of
  nature can rearrange and damage natural walkways, as
  well as sidewalks, parking lots, roads, and buildings.
  Never assume that water-damaged structures or ground
  areas are stable.

- **Don't Enter Damaged Buildings Until They've Been
  Inspected:** Don't work in or around any damaged
  building until it has been examined. Assume all stairs,
  floors, and roofs are unsafe until they are inspected.
  Leave immediately if shifting or unusual noises signal a
  possible collapse.

  Buildings marked with florescent spray paint are bearing
  symbols made by Urban Search and Rescue (US&R)
  Teams.

**Injuries or Rashes**

- **Wear Sturdy Footwear and Gloves:** The risk for injury
  during and after a natural disaster is high. Persons who
  anticipate the need to travel in affected areas should be
  advised to wear sturdy footwear to protect their feet
  from widespread debris present in these areas. High-top
  leather boots with protective toes are recommended
  when working in hazardous conditions. Never reach into
  debris piles without hand protection.

- **Take Care of Cuts and Wounds:** Tetanus is a potential
  health threat for persons who sustain wound injuries.
  Any wound or rash has the potential for becoming
  infected, and should be assessed by a health-care
  provider as soon as possible. Any wounds, cuts, or
  animal bites should be immediately cleansed with soap
  and clean water. A good preventive measure is to keep
  your tetanus booster shot up to date, or to get a tetanus
  booster at the incident location, if available.

- **Back Injuries:** Cleanup workers are at risk for
  developing serious musculoskeletal injuries to the hands,

back, knees, and shoulders. Special attention is needed to avoid back injuries associated with manual lifting and handling of debris and building materials. To help prevent injury, use teams of two or more to move bulky objects and use proper lifting techniques and devices.

**Driving**

- **Convey Your Plans:** Tell the contact person at your destination or your supervisor your estimated time of arrival and destination. Arrange for the contact person/supervisor to initiate a search along your intended route if you don't arrive within a pre-specified time limit.

- **Follow Pre-Planned Routes:** If you are given instructions to take certain routes, do not deviate. What may look like a shortcut could end up being very hazardous. Report all changes of plans.

- **Know the Hazards:** When driving in storm-impacted areas, watch with caution for confused deer, loose livestock, flooded low areas, washed-out culverts and bridges that may have undercut foundations, inoperable traffic lights, downed power lines, and debris in roadways.

- **Use Common Sense:** Know your route ahead of time. Do not use cell phones when driving. When possible, drive only during daylight hours in storm-impacted areas. Check the tires, fuel level, and condition of the vehicle before you leave.

- **Carry Emergency Supplies:** Do not begin travel unless you have enough gas, water, nonperishable food, necessary prescriptions, extra clothing, etc., to be entirely self-sufficient for 24 to 48 hours.

- **Monitor Conditions:** Continuously listen to local radio stations (not satellite stations, rebroadcast stations, CDs, tapes, etc.) for weather alerts, evacuation notifications, washed-out roads, and gasoline status information.

**Desperate Survivors**

- **Report Needs:** Unless you have the supplies and training to help survivors, report location and needs. Avoid stopping except in secure locations. If you are forced to stop, remain calm and be compliant with requests.

- **Do Not Endanger Yourself:** Do not put yourself in danger by trying to defend your belongings or vehicles. Get out of the situations as quickly as possible.

**Communications**

- **Have a Backup Plan:** Outside of incident radio coverage area, carry a cellular phone but do not depend on cell coverage being available, even in cities. Develop a backup communications plan.

# Complying With Security Measures

During a deployment, security measures to protect employees, the public, equipment, and facilities are vital to our response and recovery mission.

The Security Manager identifies any vulnerabilities and implements security measures including:

- Badge systems to protect employee personal information and sensitive equipment.
- Parking lot patrols and escorts to ensure adequate security for facilities.
- Security awareness programs and bulletins (e.g., violence in the workplace, identity theft, personal protection).

# Displaying and Safeguarding Badges

Badges restrict incident scenes and response and recovery facilities to authorized individuals and teams. Remember to:

- Wear your badge above the waist at all times while in any disaster facility.
- Remove or cover your badge when you leave the facility.
- Report all lost or missing badges to Security.

# Protecting Personal Information

As in any work location, you should take precautions while deployed to protect your personal information by:

- Never leaving valuables (e.g., purses, wallets, checkbooks, jewelry) out in the open.
- Reporting any missing property, government or personal, to the Security Group or your supervisor.
- Challenging strangers or personnel who are acting suspicious in your workspace. Ask for identification. If you are not satisfied with their answer, call for verification. It is better to be safe than sorry.

# Following IT Security Procedures

Make sure to follow your agency's information technology (IT) security procedures, including:

- Safeguarding passwords.
- Keeping your computer physically secure.
- Using your computer for official purposes only.

You will need to fulfill certain requirements prior to receiving a FEMA log-in.

# Preventing Violence in the Workplace

DHS policy is to promote a safe environment for its employees. DHS has a zero tolerance policy regarding violence in the workplace. This policy includes not only acts of physical violence, but threats, harassment, intimidation, and other disruptive behavior. Such behavior can include oral or written statements, gestures, or expressions that communicate a direct or indirect threat of physical harm.

If you observe violent or threatening behavior:

- Secure your personal safety first.
- Call 911 or other appropriate emergency contacts.
- Leave the area if your safety is at risk and you can do so without exposing yourself to harm.
- Cooperate with law enforcement personnel when they have responded to the situation.

# Summary

This lesson described accountability procedures, as well as safety and security requirements. You should be able to:

- Describe the administrative steps to take while deployed.
- Identify worker safety guidelines.
- Describe key security procedures to follow.

Next, you will learn about self-development and professionalism.

# Lesson 4:

# Self-Development and Professionalism

## Lesson Overview

A commitment to excellence throughout your deployment is an essential part of your professional responsibility.

At the completion of this lesson, you will be able to describe actions to take to promote professionalism, including:

- Maintaining positive and ethical behaviors.
- Promoting professionalism.
- Helping to resolve problems.
- Making effective decisions.
- Communicating effectively with others.

## General Ethical Principles

Public service is a public trust requiring us to place loyalty to the Constitution, the laws, and ethical principles above private gain. We fulfill that trust by adhering to general principles of ethical conduct as well as specific ethical standards. Underlying these 14 principles are two core concepts:

- Employees shall not use public office for private gain.
- Employees shall act impartially and not give preferential treatment to any private organization or individual.

In addition, employees must strive to avoid any action that would create the appearance that they are violating the law or ethical standards.

**Fourteen General Principles**

5 CFR 2635.101(b)(1-14).

Public service is a public trust requiring employees to place loyalty to the Constitution, the laws, and ethical principles above private gain.

Employees shall not hold financial interests that conflict with the conscientious performance of duty.

Employees shall not engage in financial transactions using nonpublic Government information or allow the improper use of such information.

Employees shall not solicit or accept a gift or other item of monetary value from a prohibited source unless authorized to do so.

Employees shall put forth honest effort in the performance of their duties.

Employees shall not make unauthorized promises binding the Government.

Employees shall not use public office for private gain.

Employees shall act impartially and not give preferential treatment to any private organization or individual.

Employees shall protect and use Federal property for authorized activities.

Employees shall not engage in outside employment or activities that conflict with their official Government duties and responsibilities.

Employees shall disclose waste, fraud, and abuse to appropriate authorities.

Employees shall satisfy in good faith their obligations as citizens, including all just financial obligations that are imposed by law.

Employees shall adhere to all legal authorities providing equal opportunity to all persons, regardless of their race, color, religion, sex, national origin, age, status as a parent, sexual orientation, disability, or genetic information, without retaliation.

Employees shall endeavor to avoid any actions creating the appearance that they are violating the law or the ethical standards.

# Protecting Confidentiality

Applicants for disaster assistance are protected by the Freedom of Information Act (FOIA) and the Privacy Act. Therefore, you must NOT:

- Give names of applicants to reporters seeking to interview disaster survivors.
- Verify that a specific individual has applied for assistance.
- Discuss the status of a specific individual's application.
- Discuss any information about fellow employees.

If you have any questions regarding the release of information, you should ask your supervisor or External Affairs staff for guidance.

# FEMA's Nondiscrimination Policy

FEMA's policy of nondiscrimination can be summarized as FEMA is committed to serving all individuals equally. Note that this also includes employment.

In particular:

- No qualified individual with a disability shall be denied participation in, or benefit of, any program conducted by FEMA, including employment.
- No person shall, on the grounds of race, color, nationality or national origin, sex, religion, age, disability, limited English proficiency, or economic status, be denied the benefits of, be deprived of participation in, or be discriminated against in any program or activity conducted by or receiving financial assistance from FEMA.

# Civil Rights of Disaster Survivors

We must not act with bias nor give preferential treatment to any private organization or individual.

Any time a person eligible to receive a benefit is denied equal opportunity or equal access to assistance on the basis of race, color, national origin, religion, sex, age, or disability, **that person may have been discriminated against**.

**Civil Rights of Disaster Survivors**

**1. How can discrimination happen during a disaster recovery operation?**

Any time a person eligible to receive a benefit from FEMA is denied equal opportunity or equal access to assistance as a member of one or more of the "protected groups" (e.g., race, color, etc.), that person may have been discriminated against.

**2. What is meant by the terms equal opportunity and equal access?**

Civil rights laws are based on two concepts: equal opportunity and equal access. Equal opportunity means that no one who is actually eligible to receive a benefit from FEMA should be denied that aid because of his or her race, color, religion, nationality, sex, age, religion, disability, or economic status. No one can arbitrarily decide that, for example, no Asian-Americans will receive assistance. Equal access means that once someone is determined eligible for assistance, they must actually be able to receive it…to have access to it. This means, for example, they must be able to read about the benefits in a language they can understand, or attend informational meetings in physically accessible buildings.

## 3. What are some examples of civil rights issues?

Listed below are some examples of civil rights violations, all of which actually took place in earlier disasters:

- A FEMA contractor makes racially insensitive remarks or attempts to sexually harass an applicant seeking assistance.
- A national voluntary agency provides more or better supplies to the majority population.
- An individual receives less in rental or other needs assistance than his neighbor and believes the reason is due to his race, sex, etc.
- FEMA contractors complete visits to the majority part of town before going to the minority part.
- Only minorities are housed in mobile home parks.
- Mobile home sites are poorly located, inadequately policed, etc.
- A DRC is located in an area where racial or ethnic groups don't feel comfortable or safe.
- A DRC is located in a physically inaccessible building.
- Information about assistance is not available in a language spoken by large numbers of residents.
- Local officials use Public Assistance funds to repair damage in majority areas but ignore the minority community.
- Local officials administer Hazard Mitigation Grant Program funds to provide benefits to the majority community but ignore or undervalue the minority community.
- A State attempts to set different standards for assistance to Indian tribes than to those awarded to the majority population.

## 4. What if the discrimination allegation is not against FEMA?

It makes no difference if a person alleges that their civil rights were violated by a FEMA employee or a contractor of FEMA, an employee of SBA, IRS, or any other Federal program. Any allegations of discrimination made against voluntary relief organizations are also within OER's jurisdiction. Such organizations must abide by civil rights laws when they provide services during a disaster.

## 5. What role does perception play in discrimination allegations?

There are three parts to the answer:

1. To many people, a perception of discrimination is reality. It is important to understand that disaster survivors who believe they are being discriminated against already are under enormous stress because of their experience during and after the disaster. Many have experienced discrimination throughout their lives and may be quick to assume certain actions by FEMA or the State – for example, a slow response by

inspectors, or the lack of DRCs in minority areas – means that familiar patterns have reasserted themselves.

2.  Discrimination may occur, but is unintentional. The fact that FEMA did not provide information in a certain language or didn't make a DRC accessible does not mean the Agency intended to discriminate against people with limited English proficiency or against people with disabilities. In the first case, it's possible that the DFO didn't learn about the particular language need until the operation was well advanced. In the second instance, no accessible facilities might have been available in the particular community. Our intentions aren't the issue, however: it's their impact on protected populations.

3.  Rarely, discrimination actually does happen. A contractor can say something or make a decision on the basis of prejudice, denying benefits to people who are entitled to them. Local officials can manipulate FEMA programs to disadvantage poor or minority individuals.

As noted above, FEMA isn't the only actor in the civil rights drama. Contractors, relief organizations, and State and local governments are also involved.

**6. Do I have a role in protecting the civil rights of applicants?**

Yes. If a disaster survivor informs you of an alleged violation of their civil rights, tell them to promptly call the FEMA Helpline at 800-621-FEMA (3362). The Helpline Operator will forward the allegation to the HQ Office of Equal Rights for processing. You should also contact your supervisor and your Equal Rights Officer to give them a "heads up." It makes no difference if the alleged violation happened on the telephone or in person. Don't try to argue with the individual. If someone wants to make a complaint, they have the right to do so. Remember, however, that a person asking for an appeal or re-inspection is not necessarily claiming discrimination. The FEMA Helpline Operator, in the absence of a specific allegation of discrimination, will handle such cases using normal procedures in the Individuals and Households Program.

If you have any further questions, please contact your Equal Rights Officer (ERO). The telephone number is located on the poster at the entrance to all FEMA facilities. If the ERO is no longer deployed, please call the HQ Office of Equal Rights at (202) 646-3535.

# Communicating Across Cultures

Review the following tips for communicating across cultures:

- Avoid metaphors and colloquialisms. (It's your turn at bat. As straight as the crow flies.)
- Avoid over-simplification of terms that may seem insulting.

- If a word or concept is not understood, do not repeat the same thing over again louder or slower as though the listener has a hearing problem. Reword your thoughts.
- Ask the listener to confirm instructions in their own words.
- Show concern. Acknowledge the cultural differences without bias and try again.
- Be careful of gestures and behaviors, such as touching that might be considered patronizing or might be misunderstood.
- Do not tell jokes about cultural groups, age, or gender; they are offensive and inappropriate.

# Treating One Another With Respect

To work together effectively as a team, all employees should strive to develop and maintain positive, professional relationships with coworkers and others.

The Equal Employment Opportunity Commission guidelines forbid unwelcome sexual advances, requests for sexual favors, and other verbal and physical conduct. Such actions constitute harassment when:

- Submission to such conduct is made a term or condition of an individual's employment;
- Submission to or rejection of such conduct forms the basis of an employment decision affecting such an individual; or
- Such conduct has the purpose or effect of interfering with work performance or creates an intimidating, hostile, or offensive work environment.

# Resolving Problems

The high-stress work environment at a JFO, DRC, or other field facility can affect anyone.

When you are feeling under pressure, remember to:

- Be flexible and open to change in response to new information, changing conditions, or unexpected obstacles.
- Work with others to come up with alternative solutions or strategies to address problems or needs.
- Maintain your focus, intensity, and sense of humor.
- Remain optimistic and persistent, even under adverse conditions.

# Making Decisions

One of the greatest challenges to working at a deployment is remaining calm in a stressful, fast-paced environment.

When making critical decisions, remember to:

- Confer with coworkers and supervisors as appropriate. Be flexible and open to new ideas or opinions.
- Consider the impact of a particular decision before acting on it.

# Summary

This lesson described actions to take to promote professionalism, including:

- Maintaining positive and ethical behaviors.
- Promoting professionalism.
- Helping to resolve problems.
- Making effective decisions.
- Communicating effectively with others.

The final lesson covers the check-out process.

# Lesson 5: Check-Out Procedures

## Lesson Overview

There are many reasons to finish a deployment. You may need a well-deserved break or your services may no longer be needed. Leaving a deployment needs to be done right so that others can complete unfinished business and lessons learned can be documented.

At the completion of this lesson, you will be able to describe the check-out process.

## Demobilization/Check-Out Process: Overview

When your assignment is complete you will be demobilized. Make sure to:

- Complete unfinished business and reports.
- Brief replacements, subordinates, and supervisor.
- Provide followup contact information.
- Return any incident-issued equipment or supplies.
- Evaluate the performance of subordinates.
- Follow incident and agency check-out procedures.
- Complete post-incident reports, critiques, evaluations, and medical followup actions.
- Complete all payment and/or payroll issues or obligations.
- Upon departure, notify the HR Unit.
- Upon departure, contact Deployment Unit at 888-853-9648 to check out.

## Complete Briefings

As part of the demobilization process, you should schedule a debriefing session with your supervisor to complete a performance appraisal.

If possible, you should brief the person replacing you.

## Submit Final Paperwork

Before leaving your duty station and heading home, you should take care of paperwork associated with check-out by:

- Submitting final time-and-attendance statement signed by the supervisor.
- Making return travel arrangements.
- Preparing a final travel voucher in coordination with the Cost Unit.

# Return All Accountable Property

Remember, you are responsible for:

- Properly using, caring for, and protecting all Government property (Fed Prop Mgmt Regulation and FEMA Reg 6150-1 govern).
- Reporting any loss, theft, damage, destruction, or misuse.
- Cooperating with investigations if there is lost or stolen property.
- Returning all issued equipment at check-out to the Logistics Section Accountable Property Specialist.

You may be monetarily liable if negligent in performing these responsibilities.

# Final Tasks

The final tasks in the check-out process are to:

- Clear your workstation.
- Submit after-action report entries.
- Check out through Human Resources Unit.
- Check out with Deployment Unit by calling 888-853-9648.

# Summary

Congratulations. You have now completed all of the lessons. You should now be able to:

- Prepare for deployment, including detailing what information to gather, what steps to take, and what things to pack.
- Check in when you arrive at your assigned location.
- Acclimate to the working and living conditions at the incident site.
- Take care of yourself during deployment.
- Describe the standards for accountability.
- Complete the check-out process.